More than a
Christmas Carol

More than a Christmas Carol
J.John

Cover design: Chris Jones
With special thanks to Liza Hoeksma for her editorial expertise.
Illustrations by Louise Neumann www.louiseneumann.com

Printed and bound in Great Britain by Bell & Bain Ltd, Glasgow

J.John

Illustrated by
Louise Neumann

More than a
Christmas Carol

Ebenezer Scrooge was a tight-fisted man:
hard, sharp and solitary.

He was a frosty, unapproachable figure,
avoided by everyone in the community.
But Scrooge didn't care.

All alone on Christmas Eve,
Scrooge is visited by the spirit
of his long-dead colleague,
Jacob Marley.

The spirit of Jacob is bound by the chains
that he forged for himself in life.
He is tormented in death by the things
he neglected to value.

The Spirit of Christmas Past visits Scrooge and shows him the pain and loneliness he's suffered and the times when he'd longed for the presence and warmth of friends.

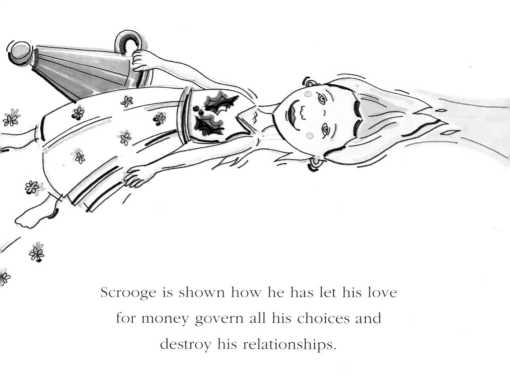

Scrooge is shown how he has let his love
for money govern all his choices and
destroy his relationships.

Our lives are full of distractions: money, status, careers, busy social calendars and possessions.

We often think of the good life as an abundance of bigger, brighter, better things.

It's easy to ignore a homeless person on the street or to change the TV channel when we see people's suffering on the news.

When we become consumed by our own desires and expectations we can become insensitive to the pain and needs of others.

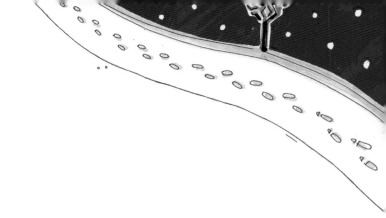

But God created us,
not to see through one another,
but to see one another through.

The Spirit of Christmas Future visits Scrooge.
The spirit has no face; he simply points towards
a time of misery when the Cratchit family have
lost their young son, Tiny Tim, through lack of
basic medical care.

Scrooge was transformed.

We can be too. Irrespective of our past,
God gives us all an opportunity to change
our future.

Scrooge helps us to pause and consider what is truly of lasting value. His story offers the hope of redemption, a better way, a brighter future.

43

At Christmas we can feel as if our hearts are bigger
– wishing peace, love and prosperity to all.

Wouldn't it be amazing if we could live with that
same love in our hearts all year round?

Charles Dickens wrote *A Christmas Carol* to communicate a message.

When God wanted to give us a message, he came to deliver it himself.

At Christmas we celebrate the birth of Jesus Christ, who lived on earth to demonstrate God's love and to show us that we can have an eternal hope.

God's love is a gift.

All we need to do is accept it and be transformed.

May God grant you;

The light of Christmas, which is faith;

The warmth of Christmas, which is love;

The radiance of Christmas, which is purity;

The righteousness of Christmas, which is justice;

The belief in Christmas, which is truth;

The all of Christmas, which is Christ.

As we celebrate the birth of Jesus,
may God grant you all these things –
not just at Christmas, but throughout
the New Year and the
years to come.

J.John Christmas Gift Books